To:

From:

On the occasion of:

THE EARTH WE SWING ON

Haiku by Raymond Roseliep

Photos by Cyril A. Reilly
and Renée Travis Reilly

WINSTON PRESS

Cover and Book Design: Evans-Smith & Skubic, Inc.
Art Direction: Miriam Frost

Printed in the United States of America
5 4 3 2 1
ISBN: 0-86683-711-6
Library of Congress Catalog Card Number: 83-60402

Winston Press, Inc.
430 Oak Grove
Minneapolis, MN 55403

Descriptively, haiku is a poem recording the essence of a moment keenly perceived, in which ideally physical nature is linked to human nature; usually untitled and unrhymed, it rarely consists of more than seventeen syllables, arranged most often in three lines, at times following a five, seven, and five syllable pattern.

The most serious Western haiku poets ... aim to use a minimal number of words to report the instant of intuition, uniting the self and the object which has moved them emotionally.... It is now up to the reader to enter into the original experience of the writer, to couple the beheld with the beholding, to identify with the "moment's monument," and to allow the captured enlightenment to lead wherever it will. As Auden and Valéry before him said of the poem, no haiku is ever finished, it is only abondoned. So the reader keeps getting on where the poet got off.

Editor's note: In the Foreword to his *Listen to Light* [Alembic Press, Ithaca, N.Y., 1980], the late Raymond Roseliep discussed the nature of haiku. The foregoing excerpt, reprinted with the kind permission of Alembic Press, is from that Foreword.

pink air
the skin
in spring

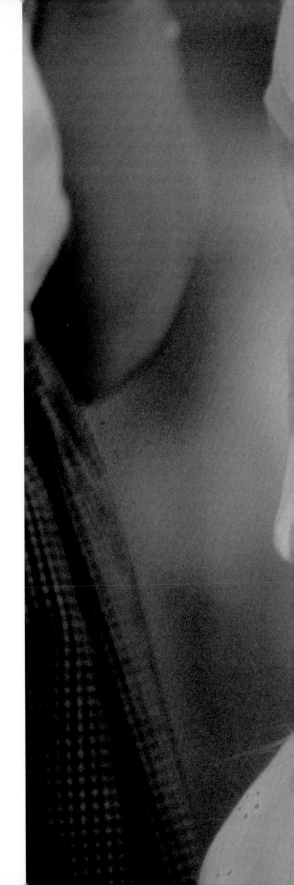

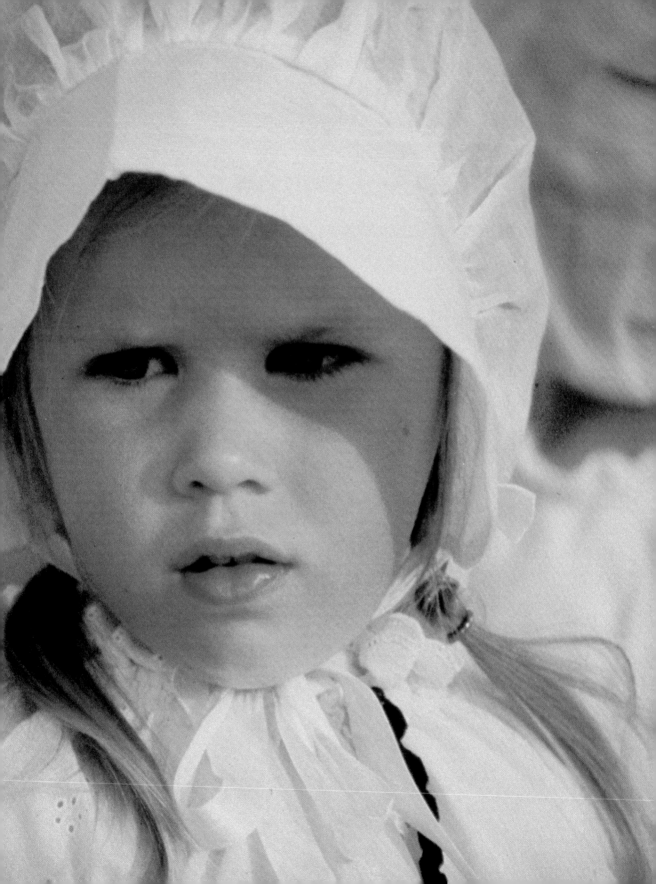

unlocking dawn
and dream:
what a key a bird is

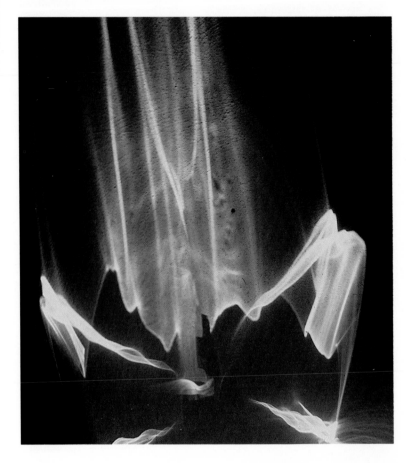

in dawn
your body
transparent

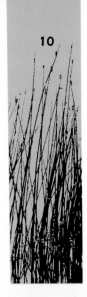

after our silence
dawn sound
is different

fleur-de-lis:
color of wood smoke,
your waking eyes

the child called
a wrong number:
we talked all spring

spring doldrums
      I phone
      the Krantz cat

dandelion gold
off in fleece
to redeem itself

by her bearing
anyone would know
she tends the rose

grass
holding the shape
of our night

shedding the clown
alone
in myself

child voice calling
  my shadow grows
  heavier

the kite pulls the boy
  till he becomes
      the air

sun beat
on drum and the earth
we swing on

the fry cook:
too busy
to hear cicadas sizzling

the child is gone
    hurry, firefly
        with your wand

on the heels of
the rainbow
flying jewels

sleep comes slowly
to my child who rides
fire-engine wings

Pied Piper's call
or Ice Cream bell—
decisions, decisions

the morning-glory
is folding more quietly
than his Morning News

bubble
catching us
   don't break

under sea gulls
some woman's pearls
birthing

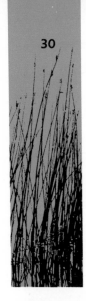

odor of earth
you catch
my breath

the farmer talks corn,
pointing where the corn
is talking

man and bee
home from work
ale on their tongues

closing the blind
against the day:
this light within

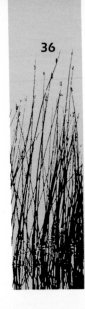

forest enough
one
leaf

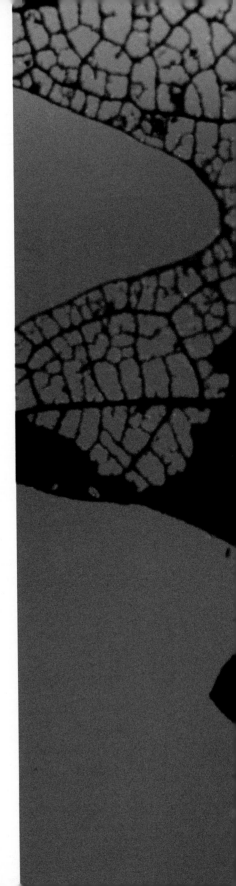

red leaf upon leaf
to measure silence
not to break it

lovers
emptying
space

dawn draws
a spider
line by line

the spider's
every eye
on its loom

touch the spider
and he makes a fist
of himself

milkweed
light flies
spun

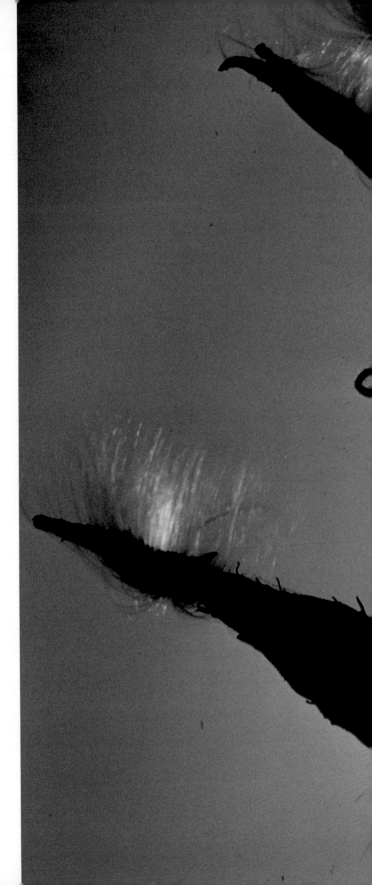

down in the swamp
bullfrogs are twanging
guitars

small frogs
learning to become
notes

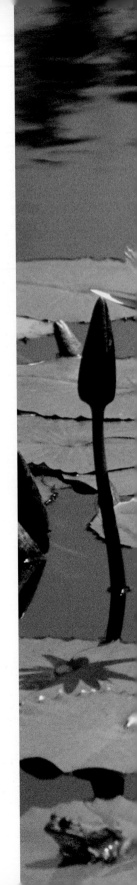

moth
on the old man's heart
both breaths flying

still life
hound
of ghost town

no one
owns
the air

in light
broken things
break

planning her quilt
grandma calls on
the giraffe

wild geese in my eyes
earth swings
off its axis

rooted
in her window chair:
leaf and leaf going

learn the river
my brother said...
egret, call him

snow holds
the soft glimmer
of their wedding fire

breath on the window
brings in the oak
with its frosty owl

winterlude:
blue breath
announcing you

old nightmare
the man's gold earring,
its eye

the storyteller
leads us children through woods
making Wolf come true

cracked bowl
that washed
her face

in snow the whisper
of my lover's footstep...
or a bird's

enough window
to light
where you were